101 Color & sing BIBLE STORIES

CREATED BY STEPHEN ELKINS

TYNDALE KiDS

Tyndale House Publishers, Inc.
Carol Stream, Illinois

Visit Tyndale's website for kids at www.tyndale.com/kids.

TYNDALE is a registered trademark of Tyndale House Publishers, Inc. The Tyndale Kids logo is a trademark of Tyndale House Publishers, Inc.

101 Color & Sing Bible Stories

Created by Stephen Elkins

Designed by Nicole Grimes

Edited by Brittany Buczynski

For manufacturing information regarding this product, please call 1-800-323-9400.

ISBN 978-1-4143-9019-2

Printed in China

20	19	18	17	16	15	14
7	6	5	4	3	2	1

Letter to Parents

101 Color & Sing Bible Stories
READ IT! COLOR IT! SING IT!

Welcome to the adventure! Truly it is! As you begin using *101 Color & Sing Bible Stories*, you'll notice that it's a little different from other children's books. Why? This book has been uniquely designed to get kids excited about reading these timeless Bible stories and exploring them in a whole new way.

We began by creating an engaging Bible storybook that's easy to read, with over 100 incredible illustrations. But that was just the beginning! We then took each illustration that appears in the book and converted it into a line-art coloring book image. This way, kids can look at the full-color illustrations in the book and enjoy coloring them in their own special way. And as they color, they can sing along with 101 favorite Bible songs—one to go with every single story—all contained on the CDs included.

Watch as your kids interact with the Bible like never before. Now they can READ about creation . . . COLOR a picture of creation . . . and SING about creation . . . all with this one amazing book! We hope you will enjoy this wonderful new expression of God's love for children!

READ IT! COLOR IT! SING IT!

How to Use This Book

1. At the beginning of each story, find the disc and song track number indicated at the top of each story page.
2. Insert the CD-ROM into your computer.
3. Print out the coloring pages.
4. Listen to the songs! You can download a handy index to all the songs at www.share-a-hug.com.

Table of Contents

God Creates the Heavens and the Earth

COLORING PAGE
Find it on the green disc!

FUN FACT
Did you know that God's tallest mountain is Mount Everest? It is 29,029 feet tall!

READ-A-LONG
Genesis 1:1-13

In the beginning, there was only darkness. But everything changed when God said, "Let there be light!" Suddenly on that very first day, God created every color of the rainbow! On the second colorful day, God made the beautiful blue sky. On the third day, He made the tall green mountains, the rich brown earth, and the deep blue sea! Everything God made was good.

SING-A-LONG

God Created
In the beginning, God created
The heavens and the earth.

6

God Creates All Living Things

COLORING PAGE
Find it on the green disc!

FUN FACT
Did you know that giraffes are the tallest animals that live on land? They can grow to be 18 feet tall! That's as high as a two-story house!

READ-A-LONG

Genesis 1:11-25

On the third day, God made all the plants and trees with leaves in every shade of green. He even made trees with oranges, apples, and bananas. Then He made flowers in every color you can imagine. On the fourth day, God made the bright yellow sun, the silvery moon, and millions of twinkling white stars. On the fifth day, God filled the oceans with fish—red fish, green fish, and even rainbow fish. He made the blue birds and orange butterflies, too. On the sixth day, God made all the land animals. Everything God made was good. But He wasn't finished yet!

SING-A-LONG

In the Beginning
Day five, He made the sparrows
And every bird that flies

And all the creatures in the sea—
God made them on day five.

God Creates the First Man

COLORING PAGE
Find it on the green disc!

FUN FACT
Did you know that God made Adam out of dust?

READ-A-LONG
Genesis 1:26–2:15

After God made all the plants and animals, God made His greatest creation: the very first person. The man's name was Adam, and God was VERY happy with what He had made! God loved all His creation, but He loved Adam in a special way. Adam was made in God's own image! God put Adam in a beautiful garden called Eden. It was a perfect home with everything he needed. God gave Adam work to do. His job was to take care of the colorful garden God had made.

SING-A-LONG

I Am Wonderfully Made
I praise you because
I am fearfully and wonderfully made.
I am a miracle heaven has made—

Glorious miracle.
That's why I praise my Father
    in heaven!

Adam Names the Animals

COLORING PAGE
Find it on the green disc!

? FUN FACT
Did you know that the African elephant is the largest land animal on the planet today?

READ-A-LONG

Genesis 2:18-20

God made every creature that walked on the ground, flew in the sky, or swam in the sea. Then God brought all the animals to Adam. Adam would give a name to every creature God had made. So one by one they came. The heavy, gray creature with a trunk, he named Elephant. The white, feathery critter that waddled, he named Duck. Adam named the big, furry animal that roared, Lion. Yes, Adam named all the animals!

SING-A-LONG

All Creatures of Our God and King
All creatures of our God and King,
Lift up your voice and with us sing,
Alleluia! Alleluia!

12

Adam Is Lonely

COLORING PAGE
Find it on the green disc!

? FUN FACT
Did you know that "worship" means to love and praise God because of how amazing He is?

READ-A-LONG
Genesis 2:18-24

As Adam named all the animals, he saw that each one had a special friend called a mate. But Adam had no helper that was right for him. God knew that Adam was lonely. So He said, "It is not good for Adam to be alone." Then God made Adam a perfect helper and friend. Her name was Eve. Adam wasn't lonely anymore! Together, Adam and Eve took care of the beautiful garden and worshiped God.

SING-A-LONG

In His Own Image
We know God made a woman,
We know God made a man.

We know He created them in His image,
Please understand.

One Simple Rule

 **COLORING PAGE**
Find it on the green disc!

? **FUN FACT**
Did you know that Satan is called "the father of lies"? (See John 8:44.)

 **READ-A-LONG**

Genesis 2:16-17; 3:1-3

God said to Adam, "You may eat fruit from every tree in the garden except one." God warned Adam that if he disobeyed, he would die. For a while, Adam and Eve obeyed God.

One day, Satan appeared in the garden looking like a snake. He must have sounded very wise. So Eve listened to him. Satan asked Eve, "Did God REALLY tell you not to eat from this tree?"

Eve answered, "Yes, He did! We can eat fruit from every tree except this one. But if we eat from this tree, we will die."

 **SING-A-LONG**

Trust and Obey
Trust and obey,
For there's no other way

To be happy in Jesus
But to trust and obey.

Adam and Eve Disobey

COLORING PAGE
Find it on the green disc!

FUN FACT
Did you know the record for the largest fruit God ever made goes to a 1,486-pound squash?

READ-A-LONG

Genesis 3:4-13

"You will not die!" Satan said. "Eating that fruit will make you like God."

Eve saw the colorful fruit hanging from the tree. It looked good to her and seemed perfect to eat. Then she remembered God's warning: "Do not eat this fruit." But believing the lie of Satan, she took the fruit from the tree and ate it. Then she gave some to Adam, and he ate it too. Oh no! Adam and Eve disobeyed God.

SING-A-LONG

Be Careful Little Eyes
Oh, be careful little eyes what you see.
Oh, be careful little eyes what you see.
For the Father up above is looking down in love,
So be careful little eyes what you see.

Good-bye, Eden!

  COLORING PAGE

Find it on the green disc!

FUN FACT

Did you know that nothing ever died until Adam and Eve disobeyed God?

READ-A-LONG

Genesis 3:22-24

Satan had tricked Adam and Eve into disobeying God. They were so ashamed of what they had done. The never-ending life God had given them was taken away. Now, they would die!

But God loved Adam and Eve. He was sad when He told them, "What you have done has caused great trouble for you and for the whole world. Now you will have to leave Eden forever." God sent Adam and Eve out of the garden. Then God put angels with a sword of fire to guard the entrance so no one could go back inside.

SING-A-LONG

Standing in the Need of Prayer

It's me, it's me, O Lord,
Standing in the need of prayer.
Not my father, not my mother,

But it's me, O Lord,
Standing in the need of prayer.

Noah Builds the Ark

COLORING PAGE
Find it on the green disc!

FUN FACT

Did you know the word "ark" means a safe place?

READ-A-LONG

Genesis 6:9-22

Noah was a good man. He loved and worshiped God. But all the other people living in the world did not love God. They never prayed or thanked God for all He had done. This made God very sad. He decided to do something He'd never done before. He would make the big, white clouds turn dark and pour down rain. God told Noah to build a big boat called an ark, because very soon the floodwaters were coming.

SING-A-LONG

Who Built the Ark?
Who built the ark? Noah! Noah!
Who built the ark?
Brother Noah built the ark.

Animals Come Two by Two

COLORING PAGE
Find it on the green disc!

FUN FACT
Did you know the ark was made of gopher wood?

READ-A-LONG
Genesis 7:1-16

As the storm clouds gathered, Noah put the finishing touches on the ark. It was higher than a telephone pole and longer than 30 cars put together! Noah had built the ark just the size God told him to make it. When the ark was finished, God told Noah and his family to load two of every animal onto the ark. How would Noah gather all the animals? God would do it! God brought all the animals to the ark, two by two. Then God shut the door.

SING-A-LONG

A to Z with Noah
We're goin' A to Z with Noah
And the animals in the ark.

40 Days and 40 Nights

 **COLORING PAGE**
Find it on the green disc!

 **READ-A-LONG**

Genesis 7:11-24

After the door of the ark was closed, the white clouds turned dark. The lightning flashed—ZOOM! The thunder crashed—BOOM! The animals were so afraid! But they were all safe in the ark, floating above the rising floodwaters. It rained for 40 days and 40 nights. Water covered the whole earth, even the highest mountains. But Noah, his family, and all the animals were safe in the ark!

FUN FACT

Did you know God creates thunder by superheating the air with lightning? Lightning always comes before thunder!

 **SING-A-LONG**

Noah's Arky, Arky
It rained and poured
For 40 long daysies, daysies . . .
Nearly drove those

Animals crazy, crazy,
Children of the Lord.

26

God Puts a Rainbow in the Sky

 ## COLORING PAGE
Find it on the green disc!

 ## FUN FACT
Did you know that a rainbow happens when light and water meet in the sky? It takes millions of raindrops for a rainbow to appear!

 ## READ-A-LONG

Genesis 8:1–9:17

Finally the rain stopped. When the land dried up, Noah, his family, and all the animals came out of the ark. It was a beautiful day! Noah thanked God for keeping them safe. God put a colorful rainbow in the sky. It was a promise that He would never again flood the whole earth. Every rainbow is a reminder of God's loving promise.

 ## SING-A-LONG

Rainbows
I have set my rainbow in the sky,
A promise I make to you, here's why:

Never again will waters rise,
For I have set my rainbow in the sky.

A Promise for Abraham

COLORING PAGE
Find it on the green disc!

FUN FACT

Did you know that there are more than 100 billion stars in our galaxy? That's too many to count!

READ-A-LONG

Genesis 12:1-4; 15:1-6

Abraham loved God and believed Him. One day God said to Abraham, "Leave your country and go to a land I will show you. I will bless you and make your family a great nation." Abraham did exactly what God said to do. He obeyed!

One night, God said to Abraham, "Look at the sky. There are so many stars, you cannot count them all! One day, Abraham, your family will be like that. There will be so many people in your family that you won't be able to count them all."

SING-A-LONG

Father Abraham
Father Abraham had many sons.
Many sons had Father Abraham.

I am one of them, and so are you,
So let's all praise the Lord!

Isaac Is Born

 **COLORING PAGE**
Find it on the green disc!

 FUN FACT
Did you know the name Isaac means "he laughs"?

READ-A-LONG

Genesis 18:1-15; 21:1-7

Abraham had a wife named Sarah. They were both very old, and they still had no children. But one day an angel came and told Abraham that Sarah would have a baby. When Sarah heard that, she laughed! It sounded impossible. But is anything too hard for the Lord? No! So when Abraham was 100 years old and Sarah was 90, they had a little baby boy named Isaac. God always keeps His promises!

 **SING-A-LONG**

Standing on the Promises
Standing, standing,
Standing on the promises of God,
   my Savior.

Standing, standing,
I'm standing on the promises
   of God.

A Wife for Isaac

COLORING PAGE
Find it on the green disc!

FUN FACT
Did you know a camel can live a month without water?

READ-A-LONG

Genesis 24:1-27

Isaac needed a wife. So Abraham sent his servant to find a bride for Isaac. The servant asked God for help. "When the girls come to get water from the well, guide me to the right one to be Isaac's wife. Let her get a drink for me and my camels, too." Just then, Rebekah came. She gave him a drink from the well. Then she said, "Here is water for your camels, too." God answered the servant's prayer! Now he knew Rebekah was God's choice for Isaac.

SING-A-LONG

Be Kind
Be kind every day,
Be kind in every way.

Be kind to each other and everyone else you know.
It's time to let your kindness show.

Twins! Esau and Jacob

COLORING PAGE
Find it on the green disc!

FUN FACT
Did you know that there are two kinds of twins? Twins that look alike are called identical twins. Twins that don't are called fraternal twins. Which kind were Jacob and Esau?

READ-A-LONG

Genesis 25:20-27

Isaac married Rebekah. News came that Rebekah would soon have a baby. But not just one baby—twins! Even before they were born, Rebekah felt them kicking each other. God told Rebekah her twins would be very different. "One will be stronger than the other. The older brother will serve the younger."

Soon the twins were born. They named the older twin Esau. They named the younger twin Jacob. Just as Rebekah had been told, the two boys were very different. Esau grew up to be a hunter, while Jacob stayed close to home.

SING-A-LONG

The Lord Is Good to Me
What a mighty God we serve!
Let's serve Him faithfully.

Jacob Gets the Blessing

 COLORING PAGE
Find it on the green disc!

 FUN FACT
Did you know that a father's blessing was so important that it could not be changed after it was given?

 READ-A-LONG

Genesis 27:1-37

Isaac grew old and blind. Knowing that he might die soon, he called for his oldest son, Esau. "Bring me something to eat," he said. "Then I will give you my blessing." So Esau went out to cook his father's favorite food.

But Jacob wanted the blessing. So he tricked his father, Isaac. Jacob put on goatskins that made him feel hairy like Esau. While Esau was still gone, Jacob came to his father and said, "I am Esau." The trick worked. Isaac gave the blessing to Jacob, the younger brother. This meant that Esau would have to serve Jacob, just as God had said.

 SING-A-LONG

Blessed Are the Children
Blessed are the children whose God is the Lord.

May He bless you and keep you,
Make His face to shine upon you.

Esau Is Angry

COLORING PAGE
Find it on the green disc!

FUN FACT
Did you know that being angry can make your heart beat faster?

READ-A-LONG
Genesis 27:41–28:5

When Esau returned and found out that Jacob had taken his blessing, Esau was very angry! He was so mad that he wanted to kill Jacob. So Jacob's mother, Rebekah, sent Jacob away to safe place. "Go to Haran, where my brother Laban lives," said Rebekah. "Stay there until Esau is not so angry. When he calms down, then you can come back." So Jacob went to Haran to stay with his uncle Laban.

SING-A-LONG

Be Quick to Listen
Everyone should be quick to listen,
Slow to speak, and slow to become angry.

Jacob's Dream

 **COLORING PAGE**
Find it on the green disc!

? FUN FACT

Did you know that some people dream in color and some people do not?

 **READ-A-LONG**

Genesis 28:10-22

As Jacob was traveling to Haran to stay with his uncle Laban, he stopped to rest. While Jacob was sleeping, he had a dream. He saw a stairway leading all the way up to heaven. The angels of God were climbing up and down the stairway. At the top of the stairway was God. He said to Jacob, "Everyone on earth will be blessed because of you. I will watch over you. I will be with you wherever you go." When Jacob woke up, he knew the dream had been a special message from God!

 **SING-A-LONG**

Jacob's Ladder
We are climbing Jacob's ladder,
We are climbing Jacob's ladder,

We are climbing Jacob's ladder,
Soldiers of the cross.

The Coat of Many Colors

COLORING PAGE
Find it on the green disc!

FUN FACT
Did you know that Joseph's coat was probably a long, colorful coat, the kind a king would wear?

READ-A-LONG

Genesis 37:1-11

Years passed, and Jacob got married and had 12 sons. One day, Jacob gave his favorite son, Joseph, a special coat of many colors. It looked like something made for a king! Jacob did not give his other sons special coats like Joseph's. So Joseph's brothers were very jealous.

God used dreams to tell Joseph about things that would happen in the future. One night Joseph had a dream about the sun, moon, and 11 stars bowing down to him. It meant that one day Joseph would rule over his father, mother, and brothers.

SING-A-LONG

Joseph's Coat of Many Colors
Many colors, many colors,
Joseph had a coat of many colors.

Joseph Is Sold to Traders

COLORING PAGE
Find it on the green disc!

FUN FACT
Did you know the pyramids of Egypt are over five thousand years old? One of them, the Great Pyramid of Giza, is one of the seven wonders of the ancient world.

READ-A-LONG
Genesis 37:18-36; 39:2

Joseph's brothers were angry with him because of his dreams and his special coat! One brother said, "Let's get rid of him." First they took away his coat of many colors. Then they threw him into a pit. When they saw some traders coming, they decided to do a very bad thing: they sold Joseph as a slave. The traders took Joseph with them to Egypt. He had to work hard, and he was all alone, away from his family. But God was with Joseph.

SING-A-LONG

My Help Comes from the Lord
God is my strength.
He is here to help me.
My help comes from the Lord!

Joseph Explains the King's Dream

COLORING PAGE
Find it on the green disc!

FUN FACT
Did you know that a pharaoh was a king or ruler in ancient Egypt?

READ-A-LONG

Genesis 41:1-36

God helped Joseph by giving him a special gift. Joseph could tell people what their dreams meant. The pharaoh of Egypt had a strange dream about seven fat cows and seven skinny cows. Joseph said God sent the dream to warn Pharaoh about what was going to happen. First there would be seven years of good crops in Egypt. Then there would be seven years when no food would grow.

SING-A-LONG

The Prayer of a Righteous Man
Powerful, mighty I say,
Powerful are the prayers we pray.

Storing Up Food

COLORING PAGE
Find it on the green disc!

FUN FACT

Did you know that some grains, like corn and wheat, can be stored for over 100 years?

READ-A-LONG

Genesis 41:37-57

Pharaoh saw how wise Joseph was. He made Joseph second in command over all of Egypt. Joseph was in charge of storing food during the seven years of good crops. Joseph did his job well. So when the time came when no crops would grow and everyone was hungry, there was plenty of food stored up in Egypt.

SING-A-LONG

Little Jobs
Whoever can be trusted
With very little

Can also be trusted
With very much.

The Brothers Come to Egypt

COLORING PAGE
Find it on the green disc!

FUN FACT
Did you know that Joseph had not seen his brothers in over 20 years?

READ-A-LONG

Genesis 42:1-8

When the years came when no crops would grow, there was no food anywhere—except in Egypt! In the land where Joseph's family lived, his brothers were hungry. So they decided to go to Egypt to buy some food.

When they arrived, they saw their brother Joseph. But they did not know it was him. He was older and was wearing Egyptian clothes. Joseph was now an important leader in Egypt, not like the helpless brother they had sold as a slave. Even though Joseph's brothers did not realize who he was, Joseph knew who they were!

SING-A-LONG

Brother, Where Art Thou?
O brother, where art thou, where have you gone?
I'm far away in Egypt, 'cause you treated me wrong.

"I Am Joseph"

COLORING PAGE
Find it on the green disc!

FUN FACT
Did you know that brothers and sisters often look alike but may act very different?

READ-A-LONG
Genesis 45:1-8

At first Joseph didn't tell his brothers who he was. He wanted to test them to see how they would act. Finally he couldn't wait any longer. He said, "I am Joseph, your brother!"

His brothers were terrified. Would Joseph be angry at them for being so mean to him?

"Come close to me," Joseph said. "Don't be angry with yourselves. It was God who sent me ahead of you and your children to save you from hunger. You meant to hurt me, but God meant it for good." God was with Joseph all along the way!

SING-A-LONG

God Works for the Good
So if God be for us,
Who can be against us?
Nobody, nobody at all!

54

Happy Day!

COLORING PAGE

Find it on the green disc!

FUN FACT

Did you know that Jacob's family would stay and live in Goshen for hundreds of years?

READ-A-LONG

Genesis 46:28-34

Joseph sent for his father, Jacob. When Jacob arrived in Egypt, Joseph gave him a big hug. What a happy day it was! Joseph's family was back together again! Then Jacob and all of his family moved to Goshen, a place in Egypt. They all lived there together for many years.

SING-A-LONG

O Happy Day!
Happy day, happy day,
When Jesus washed my sins away!

God's People Become Slaves

COLORING PAGE
Find it on the green disc!

FUN FACT

Did you know that ancient bricks were made from clay and dried in the sun?

READ-A-LONG

Exodus 1:1-14

Years passed, and Jacob's family grew. They had lots of children and grandchildren and great-grandchildren. All the people in Jacob's family were called Israelites, and they loved God just as Jacob had.

But the pharaoh of Egypt did not worship the one true God. He worshiped false gods. Pharaoh did not like the Israelites. So he decided to make them slaves. He forced them to work very hard making bricks to build his cities. God's people called to God for help!

SING-A-LONG

I Will Deliver You
Call upon Me in the day of trouble.
Call upon Me, says the Lord Most High.

Baby in a Basket

COLORING PAGE

Find it on the green disc!

FUN FACT

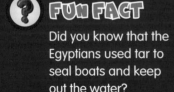

Did you know that the Egyptians used tar to seal boats and keep out the water?

READ-A-LONG

Exodus 2:1-4

Pharaoh didn't like God's people. So he passed a mean law ordering Israelite baby boys to be done away with. But one Israelite woman had a plan to save her baby boy. She made a large basket from the tall plants that grew near the river. She sealed it with sticky tar so it would float in the water. Then she carefully put her baby boy in the basket and set it among the tall grass along the riverbank. She placed her child in God's mighty hands! The baby's sister, Miriam, stood by to watch and see what would happen.

SING-A-LONG

You Will Keep Us Safe
O Lord, my Lord, You will keep us safe,
You will protect us.

A Surprise for the Princess

 ## COLORING PAGE
Find it on the green disc!

 ## FUN FACT

Did you know the name Moses means "drawn out," just like the princess drew Moses out of the water?

 ## READ-A-LONG

Exodus 2:5-10

As the baby drifted among the tall plants on the Nile River, something amazing happened! The king's daughter went down to the river to bathe. Suddenly, she noticed something floating in the water. It was a strange-looking basket. When the princess opened the basket, she found the baby boy inside! The princess looked at the baby and loved him. She named the baby Moses.

 ## SING-A-LONG

J-O-Y
Joy, joy, j-o-y. Oh, I will sing of Joy!

Miriam Obeys

COLORING PAGE
Find it on the green disc!

FUN FACT

Did you know that Moses' basket was made of papyrus, a plant that was also used to make paper?

READ-A-LONG

Exodus 2:1-9

Miriam was Moses' older sister. Her mother sent her to watch over the basket as it floated in the Nile River. Miriam obeyed and did just what her mother told her. When the Egyptian princess found the basket, Miriam spoke up. "Would you like me to find an Israelite woman to take care of the baby?" Miriam asked. The princess agreed. So Miriam ran to her mother to tell her the good news. Miriam had done her job well.

SING-A-LONG

Little Children, Obey
Obey, obey, little children,
Obey the King of kings.

Children, obey your parents
in everything.

The Burning Bush

COLORING PAGE
Find it on the green disc!

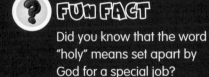
FUN FACT
Did you know that the word "holy" means set apart by God for a special job?

READ-A-LONG

Exodus 2:11–3:12

Moses grew up in the pharaoh's house. But one day he broke the law helping an Israelite slave. Moses was in big trouble! So he ran away to a place called Midian, where he became a shepherd for many years.

One day, God spoke to Moses from a burning bush. The bush was on fire, but it did not burn up! "Moses," God said, "take off your sandals. This is holy ground!" Then God gave Moses a job to do. "Go back to Egypt and tell the pharaoh to let My people go free." Moses was scared, but God promised to be with him and help him.

SING-A-LONG

How Awesome Is the Lord
How awesome, how awesome is the Lord Most High!
He is so good.

66

"Let My People Go!"

COLORING PAGE
Find it on the green disc!

FUN FACT
Did you know that there were over two million Israelite slaves in Egypt?

READ-A-LONG

Exodus 5–7

Moses went to see the pharaoh. "God has sent me here to give you a message: 'Let My people go!'" But Pharaoh did not believe in Moses' God. He would NOT let the slaves go free. Instead, he made the slaves work even harder! So Moses went back to Pharaoh and told him again, "God says, 'Let My people go!'" But Pharaoh would not listen.

SING-A-LONG

Wherever He Leads
Wherever He leads, I'll go.
Wherever He leads, I'll go.

I'll follow my Christ who loves me so.
Wherever He leads, I'll go.

The 10 Plagues

COLORING PAGE
Find it on the green disc!

FUN FACT
Did you know that God made over five thousand kinds of frogs?

READ-A-LONG

Exodus 7–12

Since Pharaoh refused to free God's people, God sent many plagues. The Egyptian people were hurt by the plagues, but not the Israelites! God kept His people safe.

There were 10 plagues in all. One of the plagues was frogs. There were frogs everywhere, in every house . . . even in people's beds! Pharaoh promised Moses he would set the people free if Moses would get rid of the frogs. Moses asked God to take the frogs away, and He did. But Pharaoh broke his promise! He would not let God's people go.

SING-A-LONG

Pass Over Me
It's called the Passover and why, you say?
While they're in Egypt-land, there came a plague.

The Red Sea Miracle

 ## COLORING PAGE
Find it on the green disc!

 ## FUN FACT

Did you know that the Red Sea is 10 miles wide where Moses and the Israelites probably crossed?

READ-A-LONG

Exodus 14

After 10 awful plagues, Pharaoh finally freed the slaves. But after they left Egypt, he changed his mind again. Pharaoh sent his huge army to catch God's people. When they saw the chariots coming, they were afraid! Pharaoh's army was behind them. The Red Sea was in front of them. There was no way of escape.

"Do not be afraid," Moses shouted. "God will save you!" Moses lifted his staff and the sea parted. God made a dry road through the middle of the sea! All God's people walked safely to the other side.

SING-A-LONG

When the Saints Go Marchin' In

O when the saints go marchin' in,
O when the saints go marchin' in,

Lord, how I want to be in that number
When the saints go marchin' in!

The Ten Commandments

Find it on the green disc!

Did you know that the Ten Commandments were written by the hand of God and not by Moses?

 **READ-A-LONG**

Exodus 20:1-17

God told Moses to go to Mount Sinai. There He gave Moses ten important rules for His people to follow. These rules were called the Ten Commandments. God wrote down the Ten Commandments on big, flat pieces of stone and gave them to Moses. God said these ten rules were to be obeyed. Why? Because they teach people how to treat God and how to treat each other! God gave us these rules to help us. He knows that if we obey the Ten Commandments, we will live safe and happy lives.

 **SING-A-LONG**

Keep My Commands
Keep My commandments and you will live.

Balaam's Talking Donkey

COLORING PAGE
Find it on the green disc!

FUN FACT
Did you know that donkeys are sometimes used to protect sheep and goats? Donkeys don't like coyotes and wolves, so they will help keep the other animals safe!

READ-A-LONG
Numbers 22–24

Some leaders from Moab offered Balaam a lot of money. All he had to do was say unkind things about God's people. Balaam started to go with the Moabites. But God sent an angel with a sword to block his path. Balaam didn't see the angel, but his donkey did. The donkey got out of the way and ran off the road. Balaam got mad and started hitting the donkey. Then God made the donkey speak! "Why do you hit me?" the donkey asked. Then Balaam saw the angel too. He told God he was sorry and went on to bless God's people.

SING-A-LONG

Building Others Up
Building, building, building others up
With a kind word or a compliment,
A friendly howdy do.

Joshua and the Battle of Jericho

 COLORING PAGE
Find it on the green disc!

 FUN FACT

Did you know the walls of Jericho were as high as a four-story building?

 READ-A-LONG

Joshua 6

After Moses died, Joshua became the new leader of God's people. They stood in front of the great walls of the city of Jericho. How would they win the battle? The walls were too tall! God told Joshua what to do. First, they would march around Jericho once every day for six days. On the seventh day, the people would march around the city seven times. Then they would blow their trumpets and shout really loud. When Joshua and the people obeyed God, the walls of Jericho came tumbling down! Doing things God's way won the battle.

 SING-A-LONG

Joshua Fit the Battle
Joshua fit the battle of Jericho,
Jericho, Jericho.

Joshua fit the battle of Jericho,
And the walls came tumblin' down!

Strong Samson

COLORING PAGE
Find it on the green disc!

FUN FACT

Did you know that Samson was so strong that he once killed a lion with his bare hands? (See Judges 14:6.)

READ-A-LONG

Judges 16

God gives different gifts to different people. Samson was given the gift of strength. He was the strongest man alive! But Samson's strength went away because he did not obey God. Soon his enemies caught him. So there he stood, tied between two stone pillars in the enemy's temple. Samson prayed, "Lord, please give me strength one more time." Then Samson pushed the pillars down, making the temple roof fall on the enemy. God answered Samson's prayer and saved His people!

SING-A-LONG

God Is Our Refuge and Strength
God is our refuge and strength,
An ever-present help in trouble.

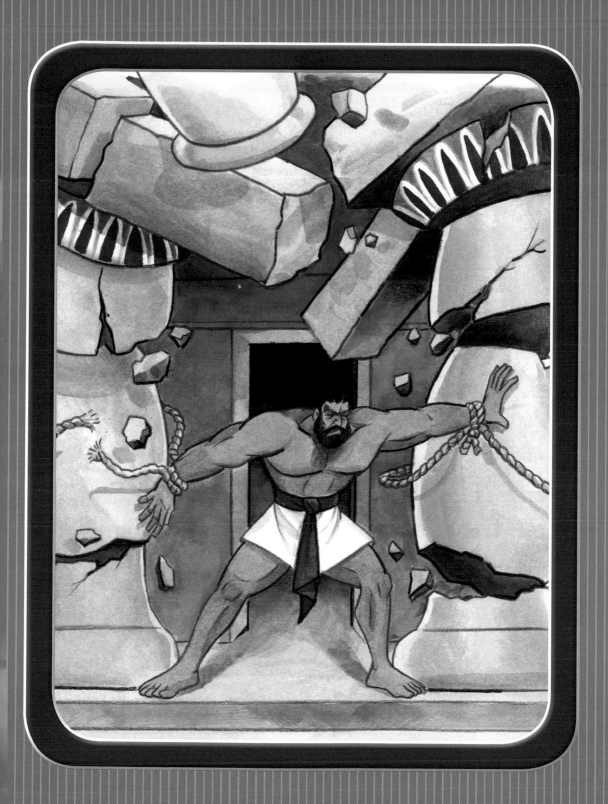

Ruth and Naomi

COLORING PAGE
Find it on the green disc!

FUN FACT
Did you know Ruth's son, Obed, was the grandfather of King David?

READ-A-LONG

The book of Ruth

Naomi and her husband and two sons moved to a faraway land. Then her husband died. Naomi's sons married women named Orpah and Ruth. But then her sons died too. Naomi was very sad and wanted to return to Israel. So she told Orpah and Ruth they could go back to live with their own families. Orpah went back, but Ruth loved Naomi and said, "Where you go, I will go. Your people will be my people, and your God will be my God." Because of Ruth's kindness, God blessed her with a husband and a baby boy named Obed.

SING-A-LONG

Where You Go
Where you go, I will go.
Where you stay, I will stay.

The Giant in the Valley

COLORING PAGE
Find it on the green disc!

FUN FACT

Did you know that Goliath's armor weighed about 125 pounds?

READ-A-LONG

1 Samuel 17:1-7

The Philistine army came to fight God's people. On one side of the hill camped the army of God. On the other side of the hill, the Philistine army prepared for battle. There was a wide valley between them. The Philistines had a big fighter named Goliath. He was a giant—over nine feet tall! He wore a suit of armor made of bronze and carried a heavy spear.

SING-A-LONG

My God Is So Big
My God is so big, so strong, and so mighty,
There's nothing my God cannot do!

Israel's Army Is Afraid

 COLORING PAGE
Find it on the green disc!

 FUN FACT
Did you know that Saul was the first king of Israel?

 READ-A-LONG

1 Samuel 17:8-11, 16

Every morning, the giant Goliath walked out into the valley and shouted. His voice was like thunder! "We don't need to have a war today," he would shout to God's army. "Just send out one man to fight me. If your man wins, then all the Philistines will be your slaves. But if I win, then you will serve us!" King Saul, the ruler of Israel, didn't know what to do. All his soldiers were terrified. Who could defeat this giant fighter?

 SING-A-LONG

When I Am Afraid
When I am afraid, I will trust in You.
I will trust in You, my Father.

The Shepherd Boy Decides to Fight

 ## COLORING PAGE
Find it on the green disc!

 ## FUN FACT
Did you know that David was probably 17 years old when he fought Goliath?

 ## READ-A-LONG

1 Samuel 17:12-32

One morning, Jesse sent his youngest son, David, to the battlefield—not to fight, but to bring a meal. David was too young to be in the army. He was just the delivery boy! He brought food to his older brothers, who were soldiers for King Saul. When David heard Goliath making fun of the Lord's army, he was mad! He said to King Saul, "Don't be afraid of this Philistine. I will go and fight him in the name of the Lord!"

 ## SING-A-LONG

The Name of the Lord
The name of the Lord is a strong tower;
The righteous run into it and are safe.

We Serve a Mighty God

COLORING PAGE
Find it on the green disc!

FUN FACT
Did you know that Philistine soldiers used swords for up-close fighting, throwing spears for medium-range fighting, and bows and arrows for long-range fighting?

READ-A-LONG

1 Samuel 17:33-37

"You can't fight Goliath!" King Saul said to David. "He is a big, strong fighter. You are only a shepherd boy. You wouldn't stand a chance!"

But David answered, "When I watched my father's sheep, I fought lions and bears that tried to hurt the sheep. I will do the same thing to this giant. The Lord who saved me from the lion and the bear will save me from the hand of this Philistine."

Finally King Saul said David could go fight Goliath.

SING-A-LONG

I'm Calling on You, Lord
Everyone who calls upon the name of the Lord
Shall be saved, shall be saved.

Goliath Loses the Fight

 COLORING PAGE
Find it on the green disc!

 FUN FACT
Did you know that the world record for throwing a rock using a sling is a distance of 1,565 feet, over a quarter of a mile?

 READ-A-LONG
1 Samuel 17:40-50
David took out his slingshot and picked up five smooth stones. He marched out and stood before the giant. "You come against me with a sword and a spear," said David. "But I come against you in the name of Yahweh, the God of Israel's army! You have made fun of God, but today He will win over you!" David put a stone in his sling and threw it at the giant. Whizzzz! The stone hit Goliath on the forehead. He fell to the ground like a big tree. With God, no enemy is too big!

 SING-A-LONG

Only a Boy Named David
Only a boy named David,
Only a little sling.

Only a boy named David,
But he could pray and sing.

Elijah's Firefall

COLORING PAGE
Find it on the green disc!

FUN FACT

Did you know that Ahab did more bad things than any of the kings before him? (See 1 Kings 16:33.)

READ-A-LONG

1 Kings 16:29-34; 18:1-40

King Ahab caused Israel a lot of trouble by worshiping false gods. So God's prophet, Elijah, said to King Ahab, "Call your priests and meet me on Mount Carmel." So 450 false prophets came to meet Elijah there. Elijah said, "You call on your god, and I will call on mine. The one who answers with fire from heaven is the true God." The 450 false prophets called out to their false god. Nothing happened. But when Elijah called out to Yahweh, fire fell from heaven and burned up everything on the altar! Elijah's God was the one true God!

SING-A-LONG

Is Anything Too Hard?
Is anything too hard for the Lord?
There is nothing He can't do.

94

Elijah's Chariot of Fire

COLORING PAGE
Find it on the green disc!

FUN FACT
Did you know that only two people—Elijah and Enoch—did not die before God took them to heaven?

READ-A-LONG

2 Kings 2:9-14

Elijah served God for many years. When he became very old, he knew that God would take him to heaven soon. So Elijah said to his helper, Elisha, "Tell me what I can do for you before God takes me to heaven." Elisha asked Elijah for a double share of God's Spirit. Elisha wanted to be close to God and feel His power. Elijah said, "You have asked a hard thing. But if you see me go into heaven, it will be yours." Suddenly, a chariot and horses of fire appeared! Elisha saw Elijah go up into heaven in a big, strong wind. Just as Elijah had promised, Elisha received God's power!

SING-A-LONG

Swing Low, Sweet Chariot
Swing low, sweet chariot,
Comin' for to carry me home.

Queen Esther Saves Her People

COLORING PAGE
Find it on the green disc!

? FUN FACT

Did you know that Esther's name means "star"?

 READ-A-LONG

The book of Esther

Esther was a beautiful Jewish girl who married the king of Persia. Her cousin Mordecai was a good helper to the king. Haman was also the king's helper, but he was very mean. Haman didn't like Mordecai, so he made a plan to get rid of him and all the Jews. Mordecai asked his cousin Esther for help. "Perhaps you were made queen for such a time as this," Mordecai said. So Queen Esther did a brave thing. She told the king about Haman's evil plan to kill all the Jews. When the king heard all this, he was very angry at Haman. Because of Esther, God's people were saved!

 SING-A-LONG

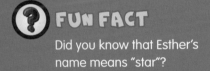

For Such a Time as This
For such a time as this,
God brought us here to sing!

The Lord Is My Shepherd

COLORING PAGE
Find it on the green disc!

FUN FACT
Did you know that shepherds sleep near the gate of a sheep pen to keep their sheep safe at night?

READ-A-LONG
Psalm 23:1

Sometimes a little word like "the" can have a big meaning. David wrote that THE Lord was his shepherd. THE Lord was the one who led him, guided him, and protected him in times of trouble. Our God is not A lord. He is not one of many lords. He is THE Lord, the one and only Lord. He is the one true God who created all things, calls us His sheep, and walks with us as our Shepherd!

SING-A-LONG

The Lord Is My Shepherd
The Lord is, the Lord is my shepherd.
How about you? Yes, He is!

I Have All I Need

 **COLORING PAGE**
Find it on the green disc!

 FUN FACT

Did you know that "faithfulness" means doing what you have promised to do? Our God is a faithful God.

 READ-A-LONG

Psalm 23:1

Because He is THE Lord, I can trust God to provide all that I need. No matter what happens, God has made a promise. He is my Shepherd, and He will give me what I need. He didn't say He would always give me what I WANT. But I can rest and not worry, knowing for sure that the Lord will supply all that I NEED!

 SING-A-LONG

Before I Ask
Before I ask, my God meets my need.
O, He loves and understands me.

He Leads Me

 COLORING PAGE
Find it on the green disc!

FUN FACT
Did you know that "trust" means believing something is true? "Faith" is acting on your trust.

READ-A-LONG
Psalm 23:2-3
Sheep are not very smart animals. They wander and get into all kinds of trouble. Left by themselves, sheep can get lost or get hurt by wolves. That's why they need a shepherd. Sheep don't know where to find grassy meadows, but the shepherd does. Sheep don't see the dangers around them, but the shepherd does. Sheep learn to trust their shepherd and depend on him. You and I are a lot like sheep. We need to trust the Lord to be our Shepherd too! He will lead us in paths of righteousness and help us do the right thing.

 SING-A-LONG

The Lord Will Guide You
The Lord will guide you.
He will take care of your need.

Still Waters

COLORING PAGE
Find it on the green disc!

FUN FACT
Did you know that following God means doing what He says in the Bible?

READ-A-LONG

Psalm 23:2, KJV

The Lord is MY Shepherd. He is the one who leads me. He is the one I depend on to help me. There are many people in the world who do not choose to follow the Lord. But I know He loves me and will keep me safe. So I choose the Lord! The Lord is MY Shepherd, and I don't need any other shepherd. Why? Because He leads me beside STILL WATERS. Sheep know that where there is still, quiet water, there is plenty of water for everyone. God promises that if I follow Him, He will lead me to a place of plenty!

SING-A-LONG

I've Got Peace Like a River
I've got peace like a river,
I've got love like an ocean,
I've got joy like a fountain in my soul!

He Restores Me

 ## COLORING PAGE
Find it on the purple disc!

 ## FUN FACT
Did you know that God can do anything?

READ-A-LONG

Psalm 23:3

Sometimes bad things happen. That's the time I need my Shepherd, who can restore me. "Restore" means to make new again. To restore something is to make it the way it used to be when it was fresh and good. If you used to be happy but now you are sad, ask the Lord for help. He can restore you. If you used to be healthy but now you are sick, ask the Lord for help. He can restore you because He loves you so much!

 ## SING-A-LONG

I've Got the Joy, Joy, Joy, Joy
I've got the joy, joy, joy, joy
Down in my heart.

The Valley, His Rod, and His Staff

COLORING PAGE
Find it on the purple disc!

FUN FACT
Did you know a shepherd uses his staff to grab hold of a sheep in danger and pull it to safety?

READ-A-LONG
Psalm 23:4

A valley can be a dark, scary place. But when sheep go through a valley, they are not afraid if their shepherd is near. They know their shepherd is watching over them. Shepherds carry two special sticks. One is a ROD. It is a straight, short stick used to keep the sheep safe from their enemies, like wolves. The other is a STAFF. It is a long stick shaped like a J. The shepherd uses the staff to guide the sheep. There's no need to fear when the Lord is with you. His rod and staff will protect and guide you along the way!

SING-A-LONG

Come Walk with Me, Lord
Come walk with me, Lord.
Come talk with me, Lord.
Come stay with me, Lord.

He Prepares a Table

COLORING PAGE
Find it on the purple disc!

FUN FACT
Did you know it takes two minutes for experts to give a sheep a haircut, and that all the wool comes off in one piece?

READ-A-LONG
Psalm 23:5-6

The Lord IS my Shepherd. He's not just GOING TO BE my Shepherd someday. He IS my Shepherd RIGHT NOW! I gladly follow Him because I know my Shepherd loves me and wants the best for me. He is preparing a TABLE for me—a wonderful, safe place with lots of food and fun things to do.

When sheep come out of the valley, they sometimes come to a flat, open space called a tableland. There, the sheep can enjoy the tall grass and play in the sunshine. God is preparing a table for us in heaven too!

SING-A-LONG

Father, We Thank Thee
Father, we thank Thee for the night
And for the pleasant morning light,
For rest and food and loving care
And all that makes the world so fair.

Train Up a Child

COLORING PAGE
Find it on the purple disc!

FUN FACT
Did you know that even mommy and daddy animals train and teach their baby animals?

READ-A-LONG
Proverbs 22:6

A soldier goes through basic TRAINING to be prepared for battle. Solomon writes in Proverbs that children need basic training too! That training prepares them for life. Training should teach three things:

1. There is a God, who created all things.
2. God loves you very much.
3. God wants you to love Him, too!

Parents should train children in this way of thinking, and children should obey. Why? Because good training comes with a promise: if children are trained to follow the right path, they will not leave it.

SING-A-LONG

Train Up a Child
Train up, train up,
Train up a child in the way he should go.

Dry Bones

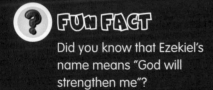COLORING PAGE
Find it on the purple disc!

? FUN FACT
Did you know that Ezekiel's name means "God will strengthen me"?

READ-A-LONG
Ezekiel 37:1-14

One night Ezekiel had a strange dream. He saw a large valley full of old, dry bones. God asked Ezekiel, "Can these bones become living people again?"

Ezekiel said, "Only You know that, Lord."

Ezekiel watched as the bones stood up, changed into real men, and became an army! Then God explained the dream. "My people are sad. Tell them they will return to the Promised Land."

Ezekiel told the people what God said. "Dry bones can live again. All things are possible with God!"

SING-A-LONG

Dry Bones
O, Ezekiel connected them dry bones,
Now hear the Word of the Lord!

Shadrach, Meshach, and Abednego

COLORING PAGE
Find it on the purple disc!

? FUN FACT
Did you know God tells us in the Ten Commandments not to worship anyone but Him?

READ-A-LONG

Daniel 3:1-15

It stood 90 feet tall and was made of purest gold. King Nebuchadnezzar treated it like a god. But it was only a statue. Statues can't love you or hear your prayers! The king told everyone that when the music played, they must bow down and worship the statue. But Shadrach, Meshach, and Abednego would not. They would never bow down to any statue or anyone except Yahweh, the one true God. When the king heard about the three men who would not obey his command, he was very angry!

SING-A-LONG

O Worship the Lord
O worship the Lord your God,
And serve Him only.

Thrown into the Fire

Find it on the purple disc!

FUN FACT
Did you know that just one candle burns at 750 degrees Fahrenheit? Imagine how hot that furnace was!

Daniel 3:14-23

The king found out that Shadrach, Meshach, and Abednego would not bow down. So he said to them, "I am going to give you a second chance. But if you do not bow down and worship my god, I will throw you into the fiery furnace!"

They answered, "We are not afraid of your fiery furnace. We fear the Lord God Almighty. He alone is able to save us. But even if He doesn't, we will not bow down."

Now the king was even angrier! He told his men to throw Shadrach, Meshach, and Abednego into the fire.

SING-A-LONG

Our God Is a God Who Saves
Our God is a God who saves,
So call upon His name.

"Now There Are Four!"

COLORING PAGE
Find it on the purple disc!

FUN FACT
Did you know that Mishael was Meshach's Hebrew name, which means "Who is like God?"

READ-A-LONG

Daniel 3:22-27

King Nebuchadnezzar's soldiers took Shadrach, Meshach, and Abednego and threw them into the furnace. The fire was so hot that it even burned the soldiers!

Suddenly, the king jumped to his feet in surprise. "Look!" he shouted. "I thought we threw three men into the fire. But I see four men walking around in the flames. And the fourth looks like a son of the gods!" So the king shouted, "Come out, Shadrach, Meshach, and Abednego!"

SING-A-LONG

The Lord Is Faithful
The Lord is faithful to all His promises
And loving toward all He has made.

The King Praises God

COLORING PAGE
Find it on the purple disc!

FUN FACT

Did you know that Yahweh is God's name, and that it appears in the Old Testament over 6,800 times?

READ-A-LONG

Daniel 3:26-30

The three men stepped out of the fiery furnace. And there they stood, safe and alive. King Nebuchadnezzar and all his servants gathered around them. They couldn't believe their eyes . . . or their noses. The men didn't even SMELL like smoke! It was a miracle. The Lord God was able to protect them from death. The king's heart was changed forever that day. "Praise Yahweh!" said the king. "And may all of my kingdom praise Him as well!"

SING-A-LONG

I Will Be Glad!
O Most High,
I will be glad and rejoice in You.

Three Times a Day

COLORING PAGE

Find it on the purple disc!

FUN FACT

Did you know that Daniel always looked toward the city of Jerusalem when he prayed?

READ-A-LONG

Daniel 6:1-10

Daniel loved God and prayed to Him three times every day, no matter what. King Darius respected Daniel and learned he could trust him to do good. So he put Daniel in charge of the whole kingdom. This made the other leaders jealous. They wanted to get rid of Daniel. So they came up with an evil plan. They tricked King Darius into signing a law that said it was wrong to pray to anyone except the king.

SING-A-LONG

Three Times a Day
Three times a day
He got down on his knees.

126

Daniel in the Lions' Den

COLORING PAGE
Find it on the purple disc!

FUN FACT

Did you know that a full-grown lion weighs over 400 pounds?

READ-A-LONG

Daniel 6:11-28

Daniel heard about the king's new law. But he kept on praying three times every day, just as before. So the bad men ran to King Darius and said, "Daniel broke your law. You must throw him to the lions!"

The king was very upset. He wanted to help Daniel, but even he couldn't change the law. So they threw Daniel into a pit full of hungry lions. He stayed there all night. But in the morning, Daniel wasn't hurt! God had sent an angel to shut the lions' mouths. God saved Daniel!

SING-A-LONG

Angels Watchin' Over Me
All night, all day,
Angels watchin' over me, my Lord.

Jonah Runs Away

COLORING PAGE
Find it on the purple disc!

FUN FACT
Did you know that Jonah sailed for Tarshish in Spain, which was the farthest city from Nineveh in the known world?

READ-A-LONG
Jonah 1:1-3

God gave Jonah a message. He told Jonah to go to Nineveh and tell the people to stop doing bad things and start following Him. But Jonah didn't want to go to Nineveh. So he decided to run away from God. But you can't run away from God—He's everywhere! Still, Jonah tried. He got on a big boat going the opposite direction. Jonah wanted to go as far away from Nineveh as he could.

SING-A-LONG

To Obey Is Better
O—It's the Only way to go.
B—Be certain it's true.
E—Everybody should obey.

Y—You and I should too.
Obey!

God Sends a Storm

COLORING PAGE
Find it on the purple disc!

FUN FACT
Did you know that before the sailors threw Jonah overboard, they threw their cargo into the sea to lighten the boat and help it float?

READ-A-LONG
Jonah 1:4-16

Jonah was trying to run away from God. But God wanted Jonah to obey Him. So God sent a great big storm to rock the boat. The winds were so strong, it felt like the boat was going to sink! The sailors were afraid, but Jonah was fast asleep. They woke Jonah up and said, "Pray to your God. Ask Him to save us!" Jonah knew the storm was his fault. He said, "Throw me overboard, and the storm will stop." So the sailors threw Jonah into the water, and the storm stopped at once. Down Jonah sank into the sea!

SING-A-LONG

God Will Take Care of You
God will take care of you,
Through every day, o'er all the way.

132

Swallowed by a Big Fish

COLORING PAGE
Find it on the purple disc!

FUN FACT

Did you know that being in the fish's belly most likely bleached Jonah's hair, skin, and clothes white?

READ-A-LONG

Jonah 1:17–2:10

As Jonah sank beneath the waves, God sent a big fish to swallow him. Jonah was in the stomach of that fish for three days and three nights! Now he was sorry he had disobeyed God. Jonah prayed and prayed. He asked God to forgive him for running away. God's love is so wonderful. God forgave Jonah and gave him another chance. The big fish burped Jonah up onto the seashore!

SING-A-LONG

Who Did Swallow Jonah?
Who did, who did, who did, who did,
Who did swallow Jo, Jo, Jo, Jo . . . ?

Jonah Prays and Obeys

COLORING PAGE
Find it on the purple disc!

FUN FACT
Did you know the city of Nineveh was so big that it took Jonah three days to see it all?

READ-A-LONG

Jonah 3

Again God told Jonah to go to Nineveh. This time Jonah obeyed. For three days Jonah told everyone there to stop doing what is bad and to start doing what is good. If they didn't listen, God would destroy the whole city! When the king and the people of Nineveh heard Jonah, they knew he was telling the truth. All of Nineveh believed God's message. They stopped their evil ways and started to praise the God of Jonah!

SING-A-LONG

Jonah's Song
Sleeper, sleeper, sleeper arise,
Call upon the Lord in your trouble.

Mary and Joseph

COLORING PAGE
Find it on the purple disc!

FUN FACT
Did you know that Jesus' name means "Yahweh saves"?

READ-A-LONG

Luke 1:26-38

There was a young woman named Mary. She was going to marry a man named Joseph. They both loved God with all their hearts. One day an angel came to Mary with a message from God. Mary was afraid! But the angel said, "Do not be afraid. God is pleased with you. He is going to give you a special baby. The baby will be God's own Son. And you will name Him Jesus." Mary was amazed! She asked the angel, "How can this be true?" The angel answered, "Nothing is impossible with God!" Mary believed and thanked God.

SING-A-LONG

What Is Impossible with Men
What is impossible with men
Is possible with God!

On to Bethlehem

COLORING PAGE
Find it on the purple disc!

FUN FACT
Did you know that it took Mary and Joseph at least four days to travel from their home in Nazareth to the town of Bethlehem?

READ-A-LONG

Luke 2:1-7

Mary was going to have a baby! But because the Roman king wanted to count the people in his kingdom, Mary and Joseph had to go to Bethlehem to be counted. When they arrived, Mary said, "It's time for the baby to be born!" Joseph looked everywhere for a place to stay. But the answer was always the same: "We have no room." So Joseph found a barn where they could stay. The barn was full of cows and sheep. But there they would be warm.

SING-A-LONG

How Far Is It to Bethlehem?
How far is it to Bethlehem? Not very far.
Shall we find the stable room lit by a star?

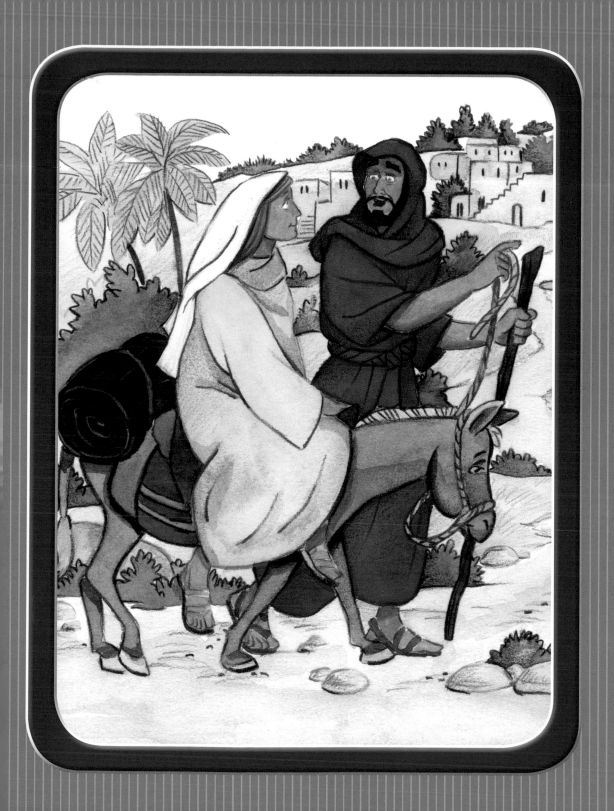

Jesus Is Born

 COLORING PAGE
Find it on the purple disc!

 FUN FACT

Did you know that the name Jesus appears in the Bible more than 900 times?

 READ-A-LONG

Luke 2:7

It was late, and Mary and Joseph were very tired from their long trip. But they had no bed or pillows waiting for them—just a barn full of hay. And Mary's baby was about to be born! The sheep and cows must have been very curious. What were these people doing here? But there in that lowly barn, with a beautiful star shining in the sky, the baby Jesus was born!

 SING-A-LONG

Silent Night
Silent night, holy night,
All is calm, all is bright.

Jesus Sleeps in a Manger

COLORING PAGE
Find it on the purple disc!

FUN FACT
Did you know that "swaddling" is wrapping babies up in soft cloth so they feel safe and happy?

 ## READ-A-LONG

Luke 2:7
Mary and Joseph were so excited that baby Jesus was born! But where would the baby sleep? They didn't have a nice crib for Him. So Mary wrapped baby Jesus in swaddling clothes and laid Him in a manger. A manger is a feeding box for animals. Just imagine: the Son of God, the King of kings, spending His first night sleeping in a feeding box for cows! But that's how much God loves us! He sent Jesus to earth to save us.

  ## SING-A-LONG

Away in a Manger
Away in a manger, no crib for a bed,
The little Lord Jesus laid down His sweet head.

144

"Glory to God in the Highest!"

COLORING PAGE
Find it on the purple disc!

FUN FACT
Did you know that the Bible says God will sing over us one day? (See Zephaniah 3:17.)

READ-A-LONG
Luke 2:8-17

Near Bethlehem, some shepherds were watching over their sheep at night. Suddenly an angel of the Lord appeared and said, "I have good news for you. Jesus, God's Son, has been born!" Then many more angels appeared. They were praising God, saying, "Glory to God in the highest and peace on earth!"

When the angels left, the shepherds said, "Let's go to Bethlehem and see this thing that has happened." So the shepherds went and found baby Jesus lying in the manger. Then they told everyone the good news: Jesus had been born!

SING-A-LONG

Hark! the Herald Angels Sing
Hark! the herald angels sing,
"Glory to the newborn King!"

John the Baptist

 ## COLORING PAGE
Find it on the purple disc!

 ## FUN FACT
Did you know that "repent" means to change? When we repent, we change our thoughts and actions to please God.

READ-A-LONG

Mark 1:1-8

John the Baptist was a prophet. His job was to get the people ready for Jesus. John lived in the desert and ate wild honey and bugs called locusts. John told the people that soon God would send the Savior He had promised. John said, "Repent!" This meant the people should stop doing bad things and instead do things that please God. Many people came to John to be baptized in the river. Getting baptized with water was a sign that they were ready for the Savior to come!

 ## SING-A-LONG

Fairest Lord Jesus
Fairest Lord Jesus,
Ruler of all nature.

Jesus Is Baptized

 COLORING PAGE
Find it on the purple disc!

? FUN FACT
Did you know that Jesus and John were related? John's mother and Jesus' mother were cousins!

📖 READ-A-LONG
Matthew 3:13-17

One day while John was baptizing believers in the Jordan River, Jesus came to him. He walked up to John and said, "Baptize me."

John knew that Jesus was the Savior, God's own Son. Jesus didn't need to repent because He was perfect! So John said, "Jesus, YOU should baptize ME." But Jesus said it was still important for Him to be baptized.

So John did as Jesus asked. Down into the water Jesus went. When He came up, God spoke from heaven and said, "This is my Son, and I love Him."

🎤 SING-A-LONG

I Have Decided to Follow Jesus
I have decided to follow Jesus,
No turning back, no turning back.

Fishers of Men

COLORING PAGE
Find it on the purple disc!

FUN FACT

Did you know that fishing nets are made in different sizes and shapes to catch different kinds of fish?

READ-A-LONG

Matthew 4:18-22

One day Jesus was walking beside the Sea of Galilee when He saw some fishermen. Two brothers named Peter and Andrew were fishing in a boat. Two other brothers, James and John, were fixing their nets. Jesus called to them, "Come, follow Me. I will make you fishers of men." At once, they left their boats to follow Jesus. They became the first disciples, or followers of Jesus. They would learn from Jesus and tell others about Him.

SING-A-LONG

Peter, James, and John in a Sailboat
A lesson they heard from the Savior:
I will make you fishers of men.

Jesus' 12 Disciples

 **COLORING PAGE**
Find it on the purple disc!

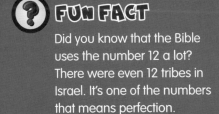 **FUN FACT**
Did you know that the Bible uses the number 12 a lot? There were even 12 tribes in Israel. It's one of the numbers that means perfection.

 **READ-A-LONG**

Matthew 10:2-4

Did you ever wonder why Jesus called His 12 closest friends "disciples"? Why didn't He give the group a fun name? They were called disciples because what they did wasn't always fun. Sometimes they had to work hard and have discipline. Discipline is doing what you SHOULD do, not just what you feel like doing. The 12 disciples were: Peter and his brother Andrew, James and his brother John, Philip, Bartholomew, Thomas, Matthew, another James, Thaddaeus, Simon, and Judas.

 **SING-A-LONG**

Come, Follow Me
We will catch them with our kindness.
We will catch them with the love of God.

Simon

Jonn

Thomas

Philip

James

Thaddaeus

Judas

Matthew

James Too!

Bartholomew

Peter

Andrew

Salt of the Earth

COLORING PAGE
Find it on the purple disc!

FUN FACT
Did you know that salt has fourteen thousand uses, more than any other mineral God created? It can preserve food, clean rust, make soap, heal bug bites, kill weeds, and much more!

READ-A-LONG
Matthew 5:13
Jesus said to His followers, "You are the salt of the earth." What did He mean? When we eat salt, it makes us want something else—water! Salt makes us thirsty. Jesus wants us to be salty people! We should live in a way that makes people thirsty for God and His Kingdom. When others see our lives, they should want what we have. What do we have? JESUS!

SING-A-LONG

You Are the Salt of the Earth
You, you are the salt of the earth. . . .
Make 'em thirsty, thirsty for the Word of God.

Light of the World

COLORING PAGE
Find it on the purple disc!

FUN FACT
Did you know that God created light to travel faster than anything else? In one second, light can go 186,000 miles! That's more than halfway to the moon!

READ-A-LONG

Matthew 5:14-16

Jesus said to His followers, "You are the light of the world." When people walk into a lighted room, there's no need to wonder what's inside. Everything is seen. But in a dark room, it's very easy to get lost. If there's no light, you can't see which way to go. Jesus said that we live in a dark world. But God's Word is like a light. When we share God's Word with others, we show them the way to find Him! It's like shining a bright light in a dark room. But if we hide our light and say nothing, our friends and family may never see Jesus. So be a light!

SING-A-LONG

Let My Little Light Shine
This little light of mine,
I'm gonna let it shine.

Seek God First

COLORING PAGE
Find it on the purple disc!

FUN FACT
Did you know that God created over ten thousand kinds of birds?

READ-A-LONG

Matthew 6:26-33

Jesus wants us to seek God first. But what does that mean? "Look at the birds," Jesus said. "They don't plant gardens to get food. Yet your heavenly Father feeds them. And look at the flowers. They don't buy clothes to wear. So do not worry about what you will eat or wear. You are much more precious to God than the birds and the flowers! God will give you what you need. So seek God first and follow Him. Then He will give you all these other things too."

SING-A-LONG

Seek First
Seek first, seek first,
Seek first His Kingdom.

The Lord's Prayer

COLORING PAGE
Find it on the purple disc!

FUN FACT
Did you know that you can pray anytime and anywhere? God always hears your prayers!

READ-A-LONG

Matthew 6:9-13

Jesus taught His disciples how to pray. We can follow the same example: "Our Father in heaven, may Your name be honored. May Your Kingdom come soon. May Your will be done here on earth, just as it is in heaven. Give us what we need today. And forgive us our sins, just as we have forgiven those who have hurt us and sinned against us. Keep us away from danger, and save us from the evil one." That's the Lord's Prayer!

SING-A-LONG

The Lord's Prayer
Our Father in heaven,
Hallowed be Your name.

Jesus Heals

COLORING PAGE
Find it on the purple disc!

FUN FACT
Did you know that Jesus used different ways to heal? Sometimes with words, sometimes with a touch, and sometimes by giving directions to do something.

READ-A-LONG
Mark 1:29-31

One day Peter came to Jesus and told Him about his mother-in-law, who was very sick. Together they went to her bed, where she lay sick with a terrible fever. Jesus reached out and gently took her by the hand. At his touch, the fever suddenly left her. She was healed by a miracle through the touch of Jesus!

SING-A-LONG

What a Friend We Have in Jesus
What a Friend we have in Jesus,
All our sins and griefs to bear!

Rooftop Miracle

 **READ-A-LONG**

Luke 5:17-26

Jesus was teaching a big group of people inside a house. It was so crowded! Four men arrived carrying their friend on a mat because he could not walk. They wanted Jesus to heal him. When they couldn't get through the crowd, they made a hole in the roof and lowered their friend down.

"Your sins are forgiven," Jesus said to the man. "Now get up, pick up your mat, and go home!" Suddenly the man felt strength coming into his legs. He stood up, picked up his mat, and walked home, praising God! Jesus had taken away his sickness AND his sin!

COLORING PAGE
Find it on the purple disc!

FUN FACT
Did you know that ancient roofs were made of clay tiles or layers of branches or straw?

 **SING-A-LONG**

Jesus Loves Me
He will wash away my sin,
Let His little child come in.

Jesus Teaches Us to Forgive

COLORING PAGE
Find it on the purple disc!

FUN FACT

Did you know that Jesus can forgive your sins? Just pray and ask Him!

READ-A-LONG

Matthew 18:21-35

Jesus told a story to teach us about forgiveness. Once there was a man who owed the king a lot of money. But he couldn't pay it back. The king was very kind and told the man he didn't have to pay him back. The king forgave the big debt! Then the man went to a friend who owed him just a little bit of money. When the friend couldn't pay him back, the man got mad. He wouldn't forgive his friend, even after the king had forgiven him! What does this story mean? Since Jesus has forgiven us for our sins, we should forgive others too!

SING-A-LONG

Forgive
We learn to live when we forgive,
Just the way that Jesus did.

Jesus Calms the Storm

Find it on the purple disc!

FUN FACT

Did you know that a very old boat was found in the Sea of Galilee a few years ago? Some people call it the "Jesus Boat" because they think it might have been His.

READ-A-LONG

Mark 4:35-41

One day, Jesus and His disciples were sailing across a lake. Jesus was very tired from teaching all day. While He was taking a nap, a terrible storm began. The wind blew harder, and the waves got bigger. The disciples were afraid the boat would sink. They woke Jesus up, shouting, "Teacher! Don't You care if we drown?"

Jesus got up and shouted to the storm, "Quiet! Be still!" At His word, the wind stopped and the waves were calmed.

The disciples were amazed. They said, "Even the wind and waves obey Him!"

SING-A-LONG

What a Mighty Hand

What a mighty hand, a mighty hand has He,
What a mighty hand that calms the raging sea.

A Little Boy's Lunch

COLORING PAGE
Find it on the purple disc!

FUN FACT
Did you know that Jesus and His disciples probably ate tilapia, which is sometimes called "St. Peter's fish"?

READ-A-LONG

Mark 6:33-44

People had come a long way to hear Jesus teach. By evening, the crowds were very hungry. Jesus asked His disciples to feed them. They said, "There is a boy who has five loaves of bread and two fish. And he is willing to share. But that's not enough to feed this many people!"

Jesus looked up to heaven and thanked God for the little boy's lunch. He broke the bread and fish into pieces. Over five thousand people ate, and there were 12 baskets of food left! A little bit goes a long way in Jesus' hands.

SING-A-LONG

Loaves and Fishes Song
Jesus took the five little loaves,
Then Jesus took the two little fish.

Walking on the Water

COLORING PAGE
Find it on the purple disc!

FUN FACT

Did you know that the Sea of Galilee is about 140 feet deep? That's like 23 men stacked on top of each other!

READ-A-LONG

Matthew 14:22-33

The disciples were rowing their boat across the lake. Suddenly a storm came up. Their boat was tossing on the waves. Jesus saw they were in trouble. So He went out to them, walking on the water!

When Peter saw it was Jesus, he stepped out of the boat to go to Him. But when Peter took his eyes off Jesus, he began to sink. "Lord, save me!" shouted Peter.

Jesus caught Peter. When they climbed into the boat, suddenly the storm stopped. The disciples were amazed. They said, "You really are the Son of God!"

SING-A-LONG

Footprints on the Water
And I saw footprints on the water,
Footprints on the sea.

174

The Prodigal Son

COLORING PAGE
Find it on the purple disc!

FUN FACT
Did you know that the stories Jesus told are called parables? He told them to teach us lessons.

READ-A-LONG

Luke 15:11-24

Jesus told the story of a man who had two sons. The younger son took the money his father gave him and traveled far away. There, he wasted all his money. So he got a job feeding pigs. He was so hungry that he even thought about eating the pigs' food. Then he thought, "I will go home and say I'm sorry. Maybe my father will let me work for food."

So he went back home. While he was still far from the house, his father saw him coming and ran to meet him, saying, "My son is home!" And he hugged and kissed his son.

Jesus' story teaches us that God is our loving, forgiving Father.

SING-A-LONG

Jesus Loves Even Me
I am so glad that Jesus loves me,
Jesus loves even me.

176

I Am the Good Shepherd

 COLORING PAGE
Find it on the purple disc!

FUN FACT

Did you know that Jesus loves you?

 **READ-A-LONG**

John 10:11-14

Jesus said that people are like sheep. And He is like a good shepherd. Sheep aren't very smart. They don't know which way to go. They get lost. That's why they must listen for the shepherd's voice. They must follow him. Jesus said, "I am the Good Shepherd. The Good Shepherd is ready to protect His sheep." Jesus loves you and will take care of you! Jesus also said, "I know My sheep, and My sheep know Me." If we follow Jesus, we become His special sheep and He watches over us forever!

 **SING-A-LONG**

I Am the Good Shepherd
I am the Good Shepherd,
And the Good Shepherd
Lays down His life for the sheep.

Let the Little Children Come

COLORING PAGE

Find it on the purple disc!

FUN FACT

Did you know that Jesus taught at the Temple when He was only 12 years old? (See Luke 2:41-47.)

READ-A-LONG

Luke 18:15-17

The boys and girls were so happy. They were going to meet Jesus! But when they came to the place where Jesus was teaching, His disciples said, "Jesus is an important man. He is too busy for children. Go away!" The children were sad.

Then they heard Jesus say, "Let the children come to me. God's Kingdom belongs to those who trust me like these children do." Jesus always has time for little children. He is never too tired or too busy. Jesus loves all the little children. And that means that Jesus loves YOU!

SING-A-LONG

Let the Little Children Come
Jesus loved all the little children.
Jesus, He loved them every one.

The Wise and Foolish Builders

 ## COLORING PAGE
Find it on the purple disc!

 ## FUN FACT
Did you know that the Bible is true and never changes?

 ## READ-A-LONG

Matthew 7:24-29

Jesus said that a wise person is like a builder who builds his house upon a rock. Rocks are strong. When it rains, rocks stay put. They do not move or wash away. So a house built on a rock will stand firm and strong. But a foolish person tries to build his house upon the sand. What happens when it rains? The sand washes away, and the house falls down!

The Bible is like a solid rock. Wise people read the Bible and do what it says. If we build our lives on the solid rock of God's Word, we will stand strong!

 ## SING-A-LONG

The Wise Man Built His House upon the Rock
The wise man built his house upon the rock,
And the rains came tumbling down.

The Mustard Seed

COLORING PAGE
Find it on the purple disc!

FUN FACT

Did you know that mustard plants love cold weather and should be planted early?

READ-A-LONG

Matthew 17:20; Luke 13:18-19

Jesus said that our faith is like a tiny little mustard seed. A mustard seed is very, very small—smaller than an ant or a grain of rice. When the little mustard seed is planted, the sun and the rain help the seed grow strong and tall. Someday it will grow into a big tree! When we start loving God, we love just a little. But as we grow, God helps us to love more and more. Then our faith grows more and more—just like a little mustard seed grows into a tall tree. Jesus said that when we have faith in Him, nothing will be impossible for us!

SING-A-LONG

The Mustard Seed Song
If you have faith as small as a mustard seed,
You can say to this mountain,
"Move from here to there."

Zacchaeus

COLORING PAGE
Find it on the purple disc!

FUN FACT

Did you know that
Zacchaeus climbed a
sycamore tree?

READ-A-LONG

Luke 19:1-10

Jesus was coming, and all the people
wanted to see Him. Zacchaeus wanted to
see Jesus too. But he was too short to see
over the crowd. Then Zacchaeus had an
idea. "I'll climb a tall tree. Then I can see
Jesus!"

As Jesus walked near the tree, He
stopped. Looking up into the tree, He said,
"Zacchaeus, come down. I will stay at your
house today." Jesus told Zacchaeus the
good news of God's love! And Zacchaeus
began following Jesus that very day.

SING-A-LONG

Zacchaeus Was a Wee Little Man
Zacchaeus was a wee little man,
A wee little man was he.

"Hosanna to the King!"

 ## COLORING PAGE
Find it on the purple disc!

 ## FUN FACT
Did you know that "hosanna" means "save us" or "Savior"?

 ## READ-A-LONG

John 12:12-15

The people of Jerusalem were excited because Jesus was coming! As Jesus rode into Jerusalem on a donkey's back, a huge crowd stood along the road. They began to sing and shout. Many waved palm branches as if to welcome a king. It was like a big parade for Jesus! Together they shouted, "Hosanna to the King! Blessed is He who comes in the name of the Lord!"

 ## SING-A-LONG

Hosanna
Hosanna, hosanna, hosanna,
Hosanna to the King!

The Last Supper

COLORING PAGE
Find it on the purple disc!

FUN FACT
Did you know that "communion" means "an act of sharing"? We still share this special meal together to remember Jesus' great love for us.

READ-A-LONG

Luke 22:7-20; John 13:34

Jesus ate a special supper with His disciples. He took some bread and thanked God for it. Then He broke the bread and shared it with His disciples. Next He took a cup of wine and thanked God for it. "Do this to remember me," said Jesus.

Then He gave His disciples a new rule. He told them, "Love each other. That's how people will know you love Me." Today we call this special meal "Communion." The bread and the drink remind us that Jesus gave His life for us. Why would He do that? Because He loves us so much!

SING-A-LONG

Do Remember
Do remember, do this to remember.
Do remember, remember what God has done.

The Cross

 ## COLORING PAGE
Find it on the purple disc!

 ## FUN FACT
Did you know that Jesus died on a hill called Golgotha, which means "place of the skull"?

 ## READ-A-LONG
Luke 23:33-48

It was a very sad day. Soldiers put Jesus on a cross. Jesus hadn't done anything wrong. But many people were angry with Him. They didn't believe He was really the Messiah as He said. So they hurt Him and made fun of Him. On the cross, Jesus asked God to forgive them. Then He died. Yes, it was a very sad day. But God wasn't finished. It was all in His plan to save us. In three days, everything changed.

 ## SING-A-LONG

The Old Rugged Cross
On a hill far away stood an old rugged cross,
The emblem of suffering and shame.

Jesus Is Alive!

COLORING PAGE
Find it on the purple disc!

FUN FACT
Did you know that Jesus' resurrection is the greatest event in history?

READ-A-LONG
Luke 24:1-9

Jesus' friends buried His body in a cave called a tomb. Then they put a big stone in front of it to seal it tight. But Jesus had a surprise for His friends. Three days later, some women went to the tomb where Jesus had been buried. They couldn't believe what they saw. The stone had been rolled away! The women saw two angels there wearing bright white clothes. "Jesus isn't here," said the angels. "He's alive!" The women were so happy and excited! They ran back to tell the others, "Jesus is alive!"

SING-A-LONG

Christ the Lord Is Risen Today
Christ the Lord is risen today,
Alleluia!

The Fruit of the Spirit

COLORING PAGE
Find it on the purple disc!

FUN FACT
Did you know that God has a special purpose just for you?

READ-A-LONG

Galatians 5:22-23

God made every tree to do something special. The purpose of an apple tree is to produce fruit: APPLES! The purpose of an orange tree is to produce fruit: ORANGES! The Bible says God has given us a purpose. We are made to produce fruit too. But not apples or oranges! God wants us to produce the FRUIT OF THE SPIRIT. Love and joy . . . joy and peace . . . peace and patience and kindness, too! Goodness, faithfulness, gentleness, and self-control . . . all these are God's kind of FRUIT: the fruit of the Spirit!

SING-A-LONG

The Fruit of the Spirit
Love and joy, joy and peace,
Peace and patience, and kindness, too.

Be an Example

COLORING PAGE
Find it on the purple disc!

FUN FACT

Did you know that little kids like you can tell others about Jesus?

READ-A-LONG

1 Timothy 2:5-6; 4:12

Paul was one of Jesus' followers. Paul wrote a letter to a young man named Timothy. Paul wanted Timothy to be an example to others and show them how to love Jesus. Paul's letter said, "There is one God, Yahweh, and one peacemaker, Jesus Christ, who stands between God and man. Jesus gave Himself as a payment for our sin. He died so we could live! Everybody needs Jesus, young people and old people. So don't let anyone look down on you because you are young." No matter how young you are, tell others about Jesus!

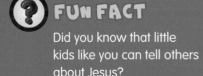

SING-A-LONG

Because You Are Young
Don't let anyone
Look down on you.

Read Your Bible

 **COLORING PAGE**
Find it on the purple disc!

FUN FACT
Did you know that the Bible is the best book ever written?

READ-A-LONG

2 Timothy 2:15; 3:16

Paul wrote another letter to his friend Timothy. In it, Paul said that everything in the Bible is true—every single verse! God has given us the Bible because He loves us and wants to teach us how to live good lives. When we read the Bible, it's like reading a message from God. What does the Bible say? It tells us that Jesus is the Messiah, the One that Yahweh sent to save us from sin. It teaches us how to treat other people. It shows us the way to heaven. Yes, the Bible is a very special book. It is God's Word!

 **SING-A-LONG**

The B-I-B-L-E
The B-I-B-L-E,
Yes, that's the book for me.

I stand alone on the Word of God,
The B-I-B-L-E.

Grow in Grace

COLORING PAGE
Find it on the purple disc!

FUN FACT
Did you know that grace is God doing for us what we could not do? He saved us!

READ-A-LONG

2 Peter 3:18

Has anyone ever sent you a reminder note? Peter wrote one to us. He reminds us that if we follow Jesus, we will never fail! He tells us to always control ourselves and be kind to those we meet. Sometimes it's hard, but we can ask Jesus to help us! As we think about all Jesus taught and as we do the things He asked, we will grow. Our hearts will get stronger, and we will become more like Jesus. We will grow in grace and in the knowledge of Him!

SING-A-LONG

Grow in Grace and Knowledge
Grow in the grace and knowledge
Of our Lord and Savior Jesus Christ.

He's Coming in the Clouds

 **COLORING PAGE**
Find it on the purple disc!

 **FUN FACT**

Did you know that when Jesus comes again, everyone on earth will see Him come?

 READ-A-LONG

Luke 24:13-53; Acts 1:6-11

After Jesus died and came back to life, He appeared to many people. He talked with two followers as they were walking on the road to a town called Emmaus. Then He visited His disciples in Jerusalem.

Soon it was time for Jesus to go back to heaven. He said, "I am going now to live with God. Now go and teach people all over the world about Me. And remember that I am always going to be with you." Then Jesus was taken up into the clouds. Suddenly two men dressed in white appeared and said, "One day Jesus will come again in the very same way."

 **SING-A-LONG**

Every Eye Shall See
Every eye shall see,
Every eye shall see Him come.

Heaven Is Real

 COLORING PAGE
Find it on the purple disc!

FUN FACT
Did you know that in heaven there will be no more death or sadness or crying or pain? Everyone will be happy! (See Revelation 21:4.)

 READ-A-LONG

Revelation 21:1–22:6

The Bible says that heaven is a very special place. It's special because it is God's home! The streets in heaven are made of gold and shine like glass. The gates of heaven are made of pearls, and the walls shine with jewels of every color. But most important, Jesus is there! People who love and trust in Jesus will walk and talk with Him in heaven forever. Their names are written in the Lamb's Book of Life. If you follow Jesus, your name will be in that book too. Heaven is a wonderful place! And Jesus is the only way to get there.

 SING-A-LONG

The Kingdom of Heaven
The Kingdom, the Kingdom of Heaven
Has been given, has been given to you.